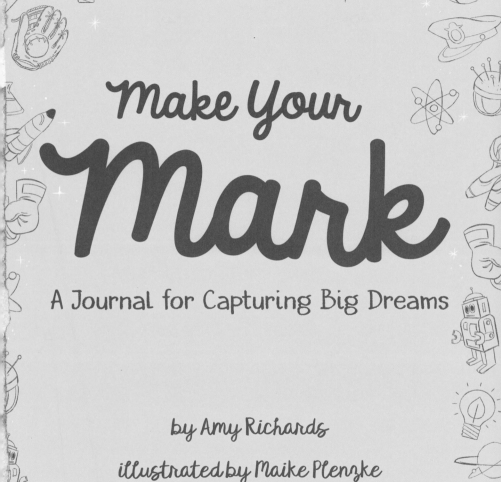

Make Your Mark

A Journal for Capturing Big Dreams

by Amy Richards

illustrated by Maike Plenzke

Penguin Workshop

A **MAKERS** Book

W

PENGUIN WORKSHOP
An Imprint of Penguin Random House LLC, New York

The publisher does not have any control over and does not assume any responsibility for author or third-party websites or their content.

Text copyright © 2019 by Amy Richards. Illustrations copyright © 2019 by Maike Plenzke. All rights reserved. The PBS Logo is a registered trademark of the Public Broadcasting Service and used with permission. Published by Penguin Workshop, an imprint of Penguin Random House LLC, New York. PENGUIN and PENGUIN WORKSHOP are trademarks of Penguin Books Ltd, and the W colophon is a registered trademark of Penguin Random House LLC. Manufactured in China.

Visit us online at www.penguinrandomhouse.com.

ISBN 9780448481791   10 9 8 7 6 5 4 3 2 1

This Book Belongs to:

_____

Who Are MAKERS?

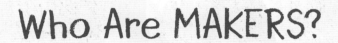

A MAKER is a woman who is doing amazing things to change the world. Some MAKERS are athletes, artists, or activists; others are businesswomen, politicians, or entertainers. They all have a passion for what they do, and they work hard to achieve their dreams. They also use their success to make sure others can succeed, too! You can learn more at www.makers.com!

In this book, you'll find stories and quotes from different kinds of MAKERS, like ballerina Misty Copeland, writer Judy Blume, and architect Maya Lin. In the "Young & Bold" sections, you'll meet kids just like you who are doing great things to improve the world. Hopefully these stories will inspire you to become a MAKER!

Misty Copeland

Misty Copeland didn't start dancing until she was thirteen years old. Most ballerinas begin much earlier—sometimes as young as three. Misty worked hard, had teachers who helped her, and after years of practice, became a ballerina with the American Ballet Theatre in New York City.

"Don't be afraid to be strong and to speak up for yourself and what you believe in. You can still be an elegant woman, and be strong and powerful at the same time."

Is there something you like doing that could turn into a career? Maybe you enjoy writing, painting, or playing a sport. Explain what you like to do and why.

_____

_____

_____

_____

_____

_____

_____

_____

_____

_____

_____

_____

Judy Blume

Judy Blume is an author who has written many books for children, like *Are You There, God? It's Me, Margaret* and *Superfudge*. Maybe you've read some of them! Judy is known for writing honestly about young people's lives.

> "[When I was a kid,] I had stories in my head all the time. I was afraid if I told anyone . . . they would think I was very strange."

> "Don't let anybody discourage you."

Have you ever made up a story in your head, like Judy? Draw or write one here.

Mae Jemison

Mae Jemison is the first African American astronaut to go into space. As a kid, she always wanted to become an astronaut, but didn't know if it would be possible since she never saw any astronauts who looked like her. Do you know what convinced her to follow her dreams? A TV show called *Star Trek* that had an African American character!

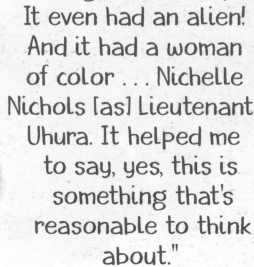

"*Star Trek* was one of our most hopeful fantasies. It had people from all around the world on the bridge of the ship. It even had an alien! And it had a woman of color . . . Nichelle Nichols [as] Lieutenant Uhura. It helped me to say, yes, this is something that's reasonable to think about."

Have you ever been inspired by a show or movie?
Which one, and what did it make you want to do?

_____

_____

_____

_____

_____

_____

_____

_____

_____

_____

_____

_____

Young & Bold

Taylor Denise Richardson

When she was nine years old, Taylor Denise Richardson was determined to become an astronaut and engineer, and raised funds to pay for her first trip to Space Camp. Since then, she has raised money for other girls to pursue their STEM (science, technology, engineering, and math) interests. She even worked with a company to create a doll based on her to inspire other girls to pursue their dreams!

"I stand for representation and equality. Let's not only break barriers, but eliminate them for a better world. Not only in STEM, but for humankind."

"I want girls to know that they can not only touch the stars, but they are already their own special and unique star."

Have you thought about going to space someday?
Draw a picture of what it might look like.

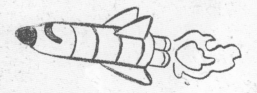

Confidence

Do you feel confident? Have you ever lacked confidence to try something new? Many MAKERS talk about the importance of having confidence:

"Confidence is everything. . . . A lot of us have . . . great skills, but who can execute when everything's on the line?"–Julie Chu, Olympic hockey player

"You have to have . . . the confidence that you're gonna be all right. You have what it takes."–Kelly Clark, Olympic snowboarder

"My confidence and courage come from something really simple: practice!"–SuChin Pak, journalist

Write five things you like about yourself. Then write five things you like about your best friend, and share them with each other.

1. _____

2. _____

3. _____

4. _____

5. _____

1. _____

2. _____

3. _____

4. _____

5. _____

Val Demings

After working in law enforcement for twenty-four years, Val Demings became the first female chief of police in Orlando, Florida. She later became a congresswoman for Florida. Quite an achievement! She says her brain is her best weapon and that she can break up a fight without putting a hand on anybody.

"Every individual living in this country has an opportunity—an obligation—to make their community, their state, this nation better."

"If you don't like something, then you do something to change it!"

If you could change something in your community, what would it be? List three people or organizations you would contact to help achieve your goal.

1. _____

_____

_____

2. _____

_____

_____

3. _____

_____

_____

Elaine Chao

Elaine immigrated to the United States from Taiwan when she was a young girl. She didn't speak English. Being an immigrant wasn't always easy, but Elaine eventually became the first Asian Pacific woman on the US cabinet (the most senior appointed officers of the executive branch of the federal government). She has had the longest term as secretary of labor.

"I believe that my upbringing made me more compassionate . . . and a better leader—and that I attribute to my parents. . . . They so believed that their daughters could achieve great things in this great country called America."

Is there somebody in your life who has supported you and/or set a great example for you? Write them a letter telling them how you feel about them. Then rip it out and give it to them.

Hooray for Moms!

Many successful women talk about the positive influence of their moms:

"I learned from my mother that if you have a chance to speak, you should speak. If you have an opinion, you should make it be known."
—Ursula Burns, former CEO of Xerox

"My mother was very . . . crucial for my success. . . . Autistic kids sometimes don't want to try something new. . . . She had a really good idea for how to stretch me."—Temple Grandin, professor of animal science, who has autism, a developmental disorder that affects how people communicate and form relationships

Do you get along with your mom? Maybe you don't have a mom, or you have two dads, or there's someone else who has helped raise you. How has that person encouraged you?

_____

_____

_____

_____

_____

_____

_____

_____

_____

_____

_____

Marlen Esparza

After winning a boxing competition when she was fourteen years old, Marlen Esparza remembers thinking, "If I can do this, I can do anything that has to do with this sport!" In 2012, after years of rigorous training, Marlen became the first woman (and one of the youngest boxers) to qualify for the Olympics—a big achievement!

"You don't have to be perfect, you just have to do what you want to do."

What have you worked hard to accomplish?
Make a list of five things you're proud of.

1. _____

_____

_____

2. _____

_____

_____

3. _____

_____

_____

4. _____

_____

_____

5. _____

_____

_____

Young & Bold
Mo'ne Davis

Mo'ne Davis was thirteen years old when she became the first African American girl to play in the Little League World Series. She even pitched a shutout game (where the pitcher pitches a complete game and doesn't allow the opposing team to score a run).

A coach discovered her amazing athletic ability when she was only seven years old. Mo'ne has played basketball, baseball, and soccer ever since. Mo'ne was the first Little League player ever to appear on the cover of *Sports Illustrated*. Her seventy-mile-per-hour pitches give new meaning to the phrase "throw like a girl"!

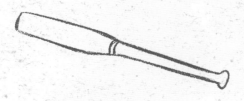

Is there a sport you like playing best? Why that sport? Or maybe you don't like sports and have another hobby. Draw or write about it here.

Linda Alvarado

Linda Alvarado is one of the first women to start her own construction company, Alvarado Construction. It builds high-rise buildings, hotels, and sports arenas. Linda is also a co-owner of the Colorado Rockies, a major-league baseball team. But she came from modest beginnings: Linda grew up in a small house with no indoor plumbing, and started her career as a groundskeeper in college.

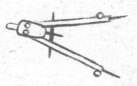

"Don't find excuses. Find reasons to succeed."

Have you ever used an excuse to not do something because you were scared or didn't think you could do it? What would you tell yourself now if you were in that situation?

_____

_____

_____

_____

_____

_____

_____

_____

_____

_____

_____

_____

Lena Waithe

Lena Waithe was obsessed with TV shows when she was a kid, especially ones that felt honest and real. She decided she wanted to write them herself . . . and she did! After working as an assistant, she now acts and writes for TV shows.

"I think there are a lot of storytellers that don't look like the storytellers of yesteryear. A lot of young, black, queer, different people that have never been a part of the culture in a mainstream way. That's the way I want to change the business . . . by helping to usher in new voices."

"The things that make me different are my superpowers."

If you could create your own TV show, what would it be about, and who would the characters be? Draw and write a story in the film strips below.

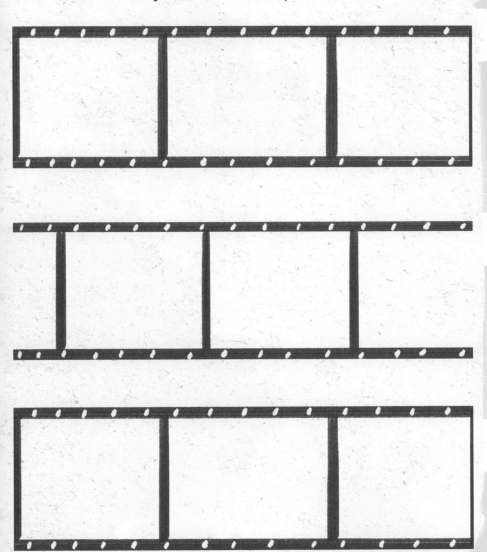

Ayanna Howard

As a young girl, Ayanna Howard loved science fiction books and anything science-y on TV. She turned her passion into a career in artificial intelligence, creating computers that can perform tasks just like humans. Today, she creates digital games that help disabled children learn better and builds robots.

"Keep proving yourself, because you're awesome."

If you could create a robot that could do anything, what kind of robot would you make, and what would it do? Draw or write about it here.

Young & Bold
Gitanjali Rao

When Gitanjali Rao was eleven years old, she won a Young Scientist Challenge award for inventing an affordable test that can detect lead in water. She was inspired to create her test because of a crisis in Flint, Michigan, where lead had contaminated public drinking water, making it unsafe to drink. Testing water for lead is usually expensive and time consuming, but Gitanjali's invention makes it much easier.

When she grows up, Gitanjali wants to be a scientist—either a geneticist (a biologist who studies genes) or an epidemiologist (someone who studies how diseases occur and spread).

If you could solve a problem with science, what problem would you tackle? How would you go about finding a solution?

_____

_____

_____

_____

_____

_____

_____

_____

_____

_____

_____

_____

Overcoming Fears

Have you ever been scared to do something, but still did it? Here's some advice from MAKERS:

"If you push through that feeling of being scared, that feeling of taking a risk, really amazing things happen."
–Marissa Mayer, former CEO of Yahoo!

"It's very healthy to be scared. I think you should do things that scare you on a regular basis."
–Glenn Close, actress

"Nobody's really fearless; it's about how you manage fear."
–Christiane Amanpour, war reporter

Sell your books at sellbackyourBook.com!

Go to sellbackyourBook.com and get an instant price quote. We even pay the shipping - see what your old books are worth today!

00008847896

0000884 7896

Is there something you'd like to do, but are scared to? Draw or write about it here.

Rebecca Adamson

When Rebecca Adamson was a young adult, she saw how badly Native Americans were treated in some schools and decided to do something about it. Her father was Swedish and her mother was Cherokee, which gave her a unique perspective on the lives of Native Americans in the United States. She helped establish schools led by indigenous people and was a leader in what is considered the civil rights movement for Native Americans.

"I come from a matrilineal society, and having women be a source of power was there in my DNA."

*In a matrilineal society, ancestors are traced through mothers (not fathers).

Do you know where your ancestors are from?
Draw a family tree, reaching as far back as you can.
Or make one up!

Ruth Bader Ginsburg

Ruth Bader Ginsburg became a justice on the Supreme Court in 1993—only the second woman on the court. She's known as the notorious RBG and has fought for equal rights throughout her life. Early in her career, her strategy was to change laws that stereotyped men and women. For instance, those that assumed men made all the money and women did all of the caregiving!

"My mother . . . had two messages for me. . . . Don't be distracted by emotions like anger, envy, resentment. These just sap energy and waste time. . . . The other was to be independent."

What are some stereotypes that you see at school or among your friends? List them, and three things you could do to change them.

1. _____

_____

_____

2. _____

_____

_____

3. _____

_____

_____

Jobs & Careers

Some people have one job their entire life, while others try out lots of different jobs. Here's some advice for figuring out what to do in life:

"If you do what you love, it's not going to feel like work."—Tracy K. Smith, poet

"You have to find something that you love doing that you feel passionately about. The success will come after that." —Michelle Rhee, education reformer

"I think that in any profession you have to learn the nuts and bolts of what you're doing, and you have to learn it over and over again and do it enough times that you've made enough mistakes to learn from those mistakes." —Katie Couric, network news pioneer

"You just have to keep at it. Nobody's career or their life is a straight trajectory up and in one direction. Everybody has had setbacks, lateral moves, problems, obstacles. That's where you learn, you adjust, you get up and keep going."—Dee Dee Myers, political analyst

What jobs have you considered having? List them here.

_____

_____

_____

_____

_____

_____

_____

Temple Grandin

Temple Grandin has spent her career coming up with ideas for how farms and slaughterhouses can treat animals better. She is autistic, which for her has meant that she is a visual thinker—she sees words as a series of pictures (autism can mean different things for different people). She believes that her way of thinking has helped her empathize with animals better. She's now a professor of animal science, as well as an author (and has countless other accomplishments!).

"You always have to keep persevering. Make yourself really skilled at something, and then, when the other people get in trouble, they're going to have to come to you because you have the answers."

Is there something you're very skilled at? How did you become skilled at it? Or is there something you'd like to become skilled at? Draw or write about it here.

Nikki Henderson

Nikki Henderson loves food and helping people, and has turned her passions into a job. She helps improve the health and economy of her community by giving people access to healthy food, whether that means helping establish a grocery store, a farmers' market, or something else. "What I do is have conversations with people to figure out what their needs are around being able to have access to fresh and healthy produce. And then I help them try to make that come true," she says.

"I love the connection between our bodies . . . health, and food, and how just changing what you put into your body can change how you feel in such a short time."

What's your favorite meal? Describe it, or make up a recipe!

_____

_____

_____

_____

_____

_____

_____

_____

_____

_____

_____

Young & Bold
Katie Stagliano

When she was nine years old, Katie Stagliano started growing a cabbage plant, which turned into a giant forty-pound vegetable. Katie donated her cabbage to a local soup kitchen, where it helped feed hundreds of people. After seeing how much one plant could do, Katie started an organization called Katie's Krops that helps kids start their own gardens to benefit hungry people in their communities.

Is there a space in your home or community where you can grow vegetables and other plants? What kinds of plants would you grow? Who could eat your food?

America Ferrera

America Ferrera's parents were immigrants from Honduras, but as a young girl, America felt very American—even though people often saw her as a Latina. She now uses her voice to advocate for what she believes in, like getting Latinos to vote and fighting for women's rights. Does she think of herself as an actress, a Latina, or the daughter of immigrants? "I don't need to have one word that sums up what I am to people," America says. "I am all of these things."

"When I have doubts . . . I look up and there's my friend using her voice . . . there's my friend doing something that terrifies her, and it helps me keep going."

What are some words/adjectives you'd use to describe yourself? Now have a friend describe you. How similar or different are the words you each used?

You:

_____

_____

_____

_____

Your friend:

_____

_____

_____

_____

Women in TV & Movies

Think about your favorite TV shows and movies. How are the female characters portrayed? Hopefully you've found shows with strong female roles.

Have you heard of the Bechdel test? It asks if a work of fiction features at least two women who talk about something other than a man. Think about your favorite books and movies, and see if they pass the test!

Do you have favorite shows or books that have strong female characters? If you can't think of any, make up a story with a strong female lead.

_____

_____

_____

_____

_____

_____

_____

_____

_____

_____

_____

Marin Alsop

When Marin Alsop was a child, she was told that girls couldn't become orchestra conductors. But that's what she wanted to do, and she didn't let anyone stop her. Marin became the conductor of the Baltimore Symphony Orchestra—the first woman conductor of a major American orchestra.

"Music has the power to change lives. It's transformative. If I can bring that to someone else, it'll be worth it."

Want to write a song? Is it funny, serious, or silly? Maybe it has the power to change people's lives!

_____

_____

_____

_____

_____

_____

_____

_____

_____

_____

_____

_____

Bethany Hamilton

Bethany Hamilton grew up in Hawaii, where she's been surfing since she was about four years old. When she was thirteen, a shark took her arm while she was out surfing. Pretty scary! She lost a lot of blood, but survived. Less than a month later, she was back in the ocean and up on her surfboard.

"I always felt invincible growing up. I was a natural athlete. . . . [I always say] look to the future, and keep on smiling!"

Have you ever dealt with a tough situation, whether it was physical or emotional? How did you overcome it? Were there people who helped you? Draw or write about it here.

Hooray for Dads!

Dads can have a huge influence over their daughters:

"My father . . . empowered me from the get-go. . . . Having that . . . affirmation of what you can do from your father . . . gives you a power that is infinite."
–Maya Lin, architect

"My father [would] tell me I could do anything I want. . . . And it has given me this insane confidence."
–Brandon Holley, former fashion editor

Has your dad been a positive influence in your life? How so? If not or if you don't have a dad, is there someone else who's assumed a fatherly role for you?

_____

_____

_____

_____

_____

_____

_____

_____

_____

_____

Vivian Stringer

Vivian Stringer was a basketball player before becoming a coach. "I could never imagine loving coaching more than I did playing, but I really did!" she says. She's her players' biggest advocate: "I'm intense. I coach through your eyes and through your heart, and I want that woman to know that she's no less than the stars in the skies." Vivian has coached more than eight hundred winning games, been inducted into the Basketball Hall of Fame, and won many awards for her coaching. Pretty impressive!

"No one can ever make you feel inferior unless you allow them. And we wouldn't allow that."

Have you had a great coach or teacher? How did they inspire you and motivate you to be your best?
If you were coaching others, what three pieces of advice would you give them?

1. _____

_____

_____

2. _____

_____

_____

3. _____

_____

_____

France Córdova

France Córdova is an astrophysicist: She uses physics and chemistry to study the nature of the sun, stars, galaxies, and more. "The big questions that we need to solve as human beings are these: [What is] the evolution of the universe, the solar system, and of life itself?" she says. France was the youngest person and first woman to become chief scientist at NASA (National Aeronautics and Space Administration). She's also passionate about encouraging girls to get involved in science.

"[Women] need role models, mentors, and opportunities to show them how exciting science can be."

What questions do you have about the universe?
List them here.

_____

_____

_____

_____

_____

_____

_____

_____

_____

_____

_____

Young & Bold
Asia Newson

When she was ten years old, Asia Newson became Detroit's youngest entrepreneur. She started Super Business Girl, a company that sells candles. "I'm the boss of this company!" she says. Asia likes helping others, too: "I teach young people like myself how to make their own money." Asia hopes to become mayor of her hometown someday, and ultimately, president of the United States.

If you were a boss, what kind of boss would you be? Strict, lenient, kind? How would you deal with successes and failures?

_____

_____

_____

_____

_____

_____

_____

_____

_____

_____

Failure

Failure isn't something to be afraid of. In fact, many women think it's something to embrace and that it helps you learn how to succeed:

"I've learned very little from success. I've learned everything from failure."–Christy Haubegger, founder of *Latina* magazine

"Not succeeding is not failure–not trying is failure."–Dee Dee Myers, political analyst

"I don't know if I believe in failures. Everything is a learning moment and it's something to grow from." –Lena Waithe, writer and actor

What have you failed at? What did you learn from the experience? Draw or write about it here.

Anna Maria Chávez

Are you (or were you) a Girl Scout? So was Anna Maria Chávez when she was a young girl, and then she became the CEO of Girl Scouts—the first Latina to lead the organization. "We aren't just about crafts, camps, and cookies. [We're] about developing future leaders of this country," she said.

"It's really Girl Scouts that sparked my imagination, and ... made me think about *How am I, as a little girl, going to change the world?*"

If you could be the leader of any organization, what kind would it be? Write five ideas here.

1. _____
_____

2. _____
_____

3. _____
_____

4. _____
_____

5. _____
_____

Reshma Saujani

Reshma Saujani is the founder of Girls Who Code, an organization that teaches girls how to code. "Coding" means creating almost anything in computer programs. Participants in the Girls Who Code programs have made things like an anti-bullying app, an app to make studying more fun, and a game using tampons. Reshma is passionate about empowering girls to pursue technology and engineering. She's especially motivated because there are many jobs that use coding skills, and girls shouldn't be left out.

"If you haven't failed yet, you haven't tried anything."

What would you create with code? An app, a computer program, a robot? What would it do? Draw or write about it here.

Positive Thinking

Do you sometimes feel sad? It's completely normal. Here are how others have found a way to get through tough times:

"Be the heroine in your life. Not the victim."–Nora Ephron, late writer and director

"Haters are my motivators." –Ellen DeGeneres, comedian

"Look to the future, and keep on smiling!"–Bethany Hamilton, professional surfer

If you or a friend is feeling down, how do you comfort each other? List five things you do.

1. _____

_____

2. _____

_____

3. _____

_____

4. _____

_____

5. _____

_____

Judaline Cassidy

Judaline Cassidy grew up in the Caribbean islands of Trinidad and Tobago, where she learned about plumbing at a trade school and fell in love with it. She's passionate about encouraging girls to develop skills, whether they decide to become plumbers, electricians, or architects, or to pursue other jobs that let them build things. She even created a group called Tools & Tiaras to help do that.

"We need to let girls start touching tools earlier. It opens up a whole new world."

If you could build anything, what would it be? A house? A hospital? An airport? Something totally new? Draw or write about it here.

Jennifer Hyman

Clothes are expensive, and many of us always want the newest thing. But keeping up with fashion trends is difficult (and expensive), so why not rent instead of buy your wardrobe? That's what Jennifer Hyman thought, and she created a company to do just that: It's called Rent the Runway.

"I am so optimistic for the future of women in business. Let's start leading by example, because the world is changing, and we're going to be the ones to change it."

"Keep on being you."

If you started a business, what would it be? Write what you would call it and what services you would offer.

_____

_____

_____

_____

_____

_____

_____

_____

_____

_____

_____

Young & Bold
Maya Penn

Maya Penn was eight years old when she started her eco-friendly fashion company, Maya's Ideas. She started by selling headbands and other accessories made of organic cotton, hemp, and bamboo. Her designs caught on, and she expanded to selling many types of clothing, jewelry, and handbags—all of which reflect her love of nature and the environment. Maya gives a portion of her profits to environmental charities and has spoken out about environmental issues in many magazines, on websites, and at public events.

If you could design any piece of clothing or an accessory, what would it be? What materials would you use? Draw and write about it here.

Limor Fried

Limor Fried loves building things and sharing her ideas and tools. As a young girl, she enjoyed "taking things apart and understanding how they worked." Now, she runs a company that helps people do just that. It's called Adafruit Industries—a manufacturing firm and global online community that gives people tools to build their own electronics.

"Engineering is saying I've got a problem, and I've got all these techniques and tools in my head, and we're going to solve this problem together."

If you could invent something in technology that would make your daily life easier, what would it be? Draw or write about it here.

Lydia Cincore-Templeton

Lydia Cincore-Templeton was bullied as a child and had to learn to stand up for herself. Her dad was her hero: "I was a daddy's girl. I was a chubby kid growing up, and he would never let anyone call me chubby or fat." As she got older, Lydia decided she wanted to help those in need, so she became an advocate for children in foster care (when children are cared for by people who aren't their parents). She started programs that have helped countless children graduate from high school.

"I felt I could be the first woman president [of the US] because of my father and my mother. They told me I could be anything I wanted, you just had to get an education."

If you could do something to help people in your community, who would you help, and what would you do? Draw or write about your ideas here.

MAKERS in Politics

Are you involved in student council or government at your school? Here's some advice from women who have served our country:

"During my campaign, every time I met a little girl, I would get down at her level, hold her hand, and say, 'My name is Elizabeth and I'm running for the United States Senate, because that's what girls do.'"—Elizabeth Warren, US senator for Massachusetts

"Take a chance. You will never regret taking a chance."—Valerie Jarrett, former senior advisor to President Barack Obama

"It's urgent for more women to be involved in government and politics. . . . Have confidence in what your goal is and what your vision is about."—Nancy Pelosi, congresswoman, first female Speaker of the House of Representatives

If you were elected to public office, what are the first five things you would do? List them here.

1. _____
_____

2. _____
_____

3. _____
_____

4. _____
_____

5. _____
_____

Ana "Rokafella" Garcia

Breakdancer Ana "Rokafella" Garcia knew she wanted to become a dancer after performing in her seventh-grade talent show. "As soon as I walked offstage I thought, 'Oh my god, I want to do this, I really want to do this!'" she says. She became a respected part of the hip-hop community and works hard to empower young people through hip-hop.

"Hip-hop is a culture. It's expression, it's freedom, and it's positive."

Have you ever performed in talent shows? What's the best performance you ever did? Draw or write about it here.

Robyn Beavers

Robyn Beavers is a sustainability pioneer, which means she finds ways to make homes and companies more environmentally friendly. For example, she installed solar panels on Google's office buildings so that they can have electricity without doing as much damage to the earth.

"Once you start thinking about the way the world works today, it becomes pretty clear that it can be designed better."

How could you make your home or school more sustainable? Maybe you could try composting, gardening, or installing solar panels on your roof. Draw or write about the things you could do.

Young & Bold
Anna Du

When Anna Du found out about microplastics—tiny particles of plastic that are harder to filter out of the ocean than regular-size plastic—she decided to do something about it. She created an underwater device that uses infrared light to detect microplastics in the ocean. Her invention led her to become a finalist in a national young scientist competition!

"I have always been interested in helping marine life and the ecosystem. Now, with the skills I have developed through this project, I know that I want to be an environmental engineer and focus not only on problems in the ocean, but also in the air and on land."

Are there environmental problems that concern you? What are they, and what are some things you could do about them?

Maya Lin

When Maya Lin was only twenty-one years old, she won an anonymous contest to create the design for the Vietnam Veterans Memorial. Some people said she was too young to create such an important monument. Others were angry that an Asian American woman won the contest. But Maya defended her design. It now stands in Washington, DC, where millions of people visit it each year.

"We are here to try to make the world a better place."

How do you think you can make the world a better place? Write three things you can do.

1. _____

_____

_____

2. _____

_____

_____

3. _____

_____

_____

Shelly Lazarus

Shelly Lazarus is an advertising executive. She helped create the Dove beauty campaign that featured women of all sizes, shapes, and ages. Her work was unusual and hit a nerve. Hopefully more ads will represent women realistically in years ahead.

"[We] set out to . . . start a dialogue about what is real beauty."

"The great thing about living in this age is that women are allowed to have any ambition that they can dream of. If you can dream it, you can do it!"

Design an ad for one of your favorite things, such as a food, a game, or a piece of clothing.

Jenette Kahn

Jenette Kahn grew up reading comic books. After being the publisher of several magazines, she became the president of DC Comics. She remembers thinking that "Batman seemed like a dark, obsessed artist. He didn't have any special powers, but he transformed himself into a superhero. I thought, 'If he can do it, I can do it, too!'"

"Women should gravitate to power. If your heart is in the right place, if you have a moral compass, you can affect really positive change."

Create your own comic strip. Who's your hero, and what's their mission?

Young & Bold
Mary Grace Henry

For her twelfth birthday, Mary Grace Henry wanted a sewing machine. Her goal was to make headbands to sell, and to use the money to help girls and boys in impoverished countries have access to education. She founded Reverse the Course, and as of 2018, she has helped 115 girls in four countries get an education.

"The very best tool that would give someone a real chance was one she could use to pursue her own dreams: an education."

Do you think the education you're getting will help you later in life? What are your favorite subjects in school?

_____

_____

_____

_____

_____

_____

_____

_____

_____

_____

Business

If you've ever considered a job in business, here's some advice:

"Be curious about everything. I'm talking about intellectual curiosity. Dig deep. Be curious. Have an insatiability to find out what's really going on."
–Indra Nooyi, former CEO of PepsiCo

"You can't sit back and wait for the story to come to you, you have to go pursue it. Dig, push, and be bold!"
–Connie Chung, former CBS news anchor

Have you ever done something in business, like selling lemonade or tickets for a school dance? Was it successful? Would you do anything differently next time? Draw or write about it here.

Shonda Rhimes

Shonda Rhimes is a screenwriter and producer whose shows feature smart, strong, and flawed female characters. "I'm not writing a fairy tale where everything's perfect. And I'm proud of that!" she says.

"I'm a highly competitive person. It's always made me want to be the best in my class or the smartest person doing something, or work the hardest. I like to be really good at what I'm doing."

"I define *feminist* as someone who gets equal pay and equal rights for the work that they do both at home and at the office. . . . [It's] a very strong, interesting, and clean word."

Do you consider yourself a feminist? What does that mean to you?

_____

_____

_____

_____

_____

_____

_____

_____

_____

_____

_____

Priya Haji

Have you heard of socially responsible companies? It means companies that balance making money with activities that benefit society. Priya likes to find out what people's challenges and struggles are, and then she thinks of ways to use business or technology to try to solve their problems.

"I really think the best ideas are still out there. If you know you have one of them, don't doubt yourself—just try."

What is a cause you care about, and what three things can you do to fight for it?

1. _____

_____

_____

2. _____

_____

_____

3. _____

_____

_____

Gloria Steinem

Have you heard of Gloria Steinem? She's considered a leader of the feminist movement. She's a writer and activist, and has spent her career fighting for women's rights. She has inspired many other women to fight for what they believe in.

"Practically all big change starts with small groups."

Name five women who inspire you, and explain why.

1. _____

_____

2. _____

_____

3. _____

_____

4. _____

_____

5. _____

_____

And here's the most important question of all: How will you become someone who inspires others? What impact do you want to have on the world? Write five things you want to accomplish in the next month to reach your goal, and explain how you will achieve them.

Find out more about MAKERS!

MAKERS started as a documentary film about women in America, but soon the creators collected so many great stories that they realized one film wouldn't be enough. They've created a growing online archive of over 400 women's stories, and have made over eight films about women's impact on the world.

It's important to celebrate these women (and a few men) who aren't always included in traditional history. Their example is the best motivation for you to make your own mark on the world.

To watch interviews with the MAKERS featured in this book (and others!) and the MAKERS documentaries, go to *www.makers.com*. Check out the MAKERS blog, too, *www.makers.com/blog*, and MAKERS on Facebook, Twitter, Instagram, Pinterest, and Tumblr.

About the Author

Amy Richards is an advisor for MAKERS, a producer of Viceland's *WOMAN*, and a co-author of *Manifesta: Young Women, Feminism, and the Future*. A co-founder of the Third Wave, Amy is also the president of Soapbox, which manages dozens of thought leaders, and hosts the popular Feminist Camps.

Sources for Young & Bold

Taylor Denise Richardson: *https://www.youtube.com/watch?v=j9-83Ygxmtk*

Mo'ne Davis: *https://www.si.com/more-sports/2014/08/19/mone-davis-little-league-world-series-sports-illustrated-cover*

Gitanjali Rao: *https://www.cnn.com/2017/11/28/health/gitanjali-rao-young-scientist-winner/index.html*

Katie Stagliano: *http://katieskrops.com/*

Asia Newson: *https://www.forbes.com/sites/leahhunter/2017/01/10/the-13-year-old-entrepreneur-changing-the-face-of-business-in-detroit/#17452c7c1f1d*

Maya Penn: *http://grist.org/people/this-14-year-old-will-fix-the-planet-before-she-graduates/*

Anna Du: *https://amysmartgirls.com/meet-13-year-old-anna-du-2018-discovery-education-3m-young-scientist-challenge-finalist-12ba2006f2fa*

Mary Grace Henry: *http://www.reversethecourse.org/impact/*